Get On Board the New Underground Railroad

Harriet Tubman's Spirit is Guiding Us to Love In Actions

Karol V. Brown-Jones

Brown Tones Publishing

Book Cover by SORA AI

1st edition 2025

Contents

1. Introduction – Guided by Spirit, Inspired by Synchronicity 1
2. Planting Seeds of Self-Love and Unity 6
3. The New Underground Railroad 16
4. Self-Love and Freedom 22
5. Prayers and Connections 26
6. Faith and Foresight 31
7. Love in Actions: Faith That Moves 38
8. Love and Compassion in Action 44
9. Eternal Life and Legacy 49
10. Love In Actions 56
11. Living Forward in Love In Actions 61
12. GG gets an Upgrade 65
13. Epilogue: Love in Actions Lives On 72
14. Moving Forward Together on the New Underground Railroad 75

Chapter One

Introduction – Guided by Spirit, Inspired by Synchronicity

On August 26, 2025, I attended a virtual women's networking meeting organization started by Adora Crystal Evans, the DIVA Network—Driven, Inspiring, Visionary, Authentic, Sisterhood. On this day, Alexandra Silva Labarr spoke about her new book, Show Up Scared, and invited us to consider, "What fears are holding you back?" I found myself thinking about her question for the rest of the week.

That next Sunday, I went to Unity of Olympia Church. Rev. Terry Murray and I had already talked about me speaking in September, when the church's theme would be Synchronicities. During her sermon, Rev. Terry spoke about prayer and taking action.

Both Alexandra and Rev. Terry touched my heart—one challenged me to face my fears, the other inspired me to act.

Truthfully, I was scared to write a book about myself and my personal stories. My intuition nudged me to share, but fear was slowing me down. Hearing Rev. Terry talk about love and action reminded me of my business phrase, **Love In Actions**. That morning, driving forty minutes to church, I listened to a Napoleon Hill podcast about building a positive mental attitude. He spoke about facing fears and believing in yourself. By the time I got home, everything felt in alignment, and I knew I had to start writing this book.

Looking back over seventy-two years, my life feels like

a puzzle, each piece shaped by moments of synchronicity, when God's gentle hand guided me to places and people I could never have imagined would be a part of my story.

For over twenty-five years, I have portrayed Harriet Tubman, a woman who trusted God completely and expressed her love through bold, compassionate actions. Wearing her shawl and telling her story prepared me for something deeper. Through Harriet, I learned that faith in action is transformative, and that love when embodied in our choices, creates real change.

Love In Actions mean choosing love as a guide for every thought, word, and action—showing compassion, unity, and care in our daily life. **Love In Actions** means being bold with kindness, standing for justice, and letting our caring for ourselves, and others become a force that heals, empowers, and restores.

I have found that the heart of every faith tradition is a call to love, dignity, compassion, and unity. Though my knowledge on religions is limited, my faith is deep, and my desire to learn is relentless. When I reflect on these universal truths, I see that what unites us is greater than what divides us.

Each chapter in this book was inspired by moments of synchronicity, unexpected conversations, quiet revelations, and ordinary miracles that showed me I was on the right path. As I look back and reflect on these conversations and people along the path, I call them my Earth Angels. For example, a wonderful guest I interviewed for my podcast, GG United By Love, Camille L. Miller, who I met through DIVA Network, told me,

"When we admire traits in others, it's because those same traits live within us."

Hearing this made me realize all those years spent with Harriet were not just educational, they were a mirror, showing me my own courage, commitment, and the legacy I am called to live.

With every page, I hope to share the synchronicities that shaped this journey, and how each one inspired me to launch my true purpose: to bring people together in **Love In Actions**, just as the Underground Railroad once did.

The Underground Railroad was never about trains or tunnels underground. It was a movement sustained by people helping others—ordinary individuals who acted out of love and unity, risking their safety and freedom for the sake of others. These people were guided by something deeper than rules or fear. They lived true to their conscience and God's truth, honoring the teachings that call us to love, dignity, and justice. Courageous souls—conductors, stationmasters, and supporters—were united by the conviction that all people deserve to be free. Every safe house, every compassionate gesture, every mile walked in darkness was powered by **Love In Actions**. They believed in the "greater good" and let spiritual truth guide their choices, showing that unity and love are the ultimate sources of real change and freedom.

Being seventy-two means I have a lifetime of experiences behind me. To some, this age means slowing down, retiring, and spoiling grandchildren. I believe every stage of life is ripe for change and possibility. These years have proven that no matter how old you are—you can continue to find joy and make a difference.

This is my third book, but for the first time, I am sharing not just Harriet Tubman's story, but mine as well. My reflections are shaped by spiritual guidance—how God has directed my steps, revealing courage, truth, and freedom I once didn't know I possessed.

As a storyteller, I have always enjoyed teaching through stories, though I rarely shared much about myself. But there comes a time when we must look in the mirror and ask: What am I truly here to do? What is my purpose?

This book was born out of moments that felt divinely orchestrated. As you read, I invite you to notice them with me. Again and again, I am led to a clear purpose: to teach and embody self-love.

My previous books carried this message through Harriet's story—30 Lessons in Love, Leadership, and Legacy from Harriet Tubman, and The Harriet Tubman Way: An Inspirational Guide to Self-Love, Empowerment, and Legendary Leadership for Girls. Harriet's life is a roadmap of faith, courage, and love for all of us, of all ages.

Today, I see my own stories reflect the same truths. My life is different from Harriet's, but the lessons remain. We need modern-day "Harriet Tubmans"—people willing to live with faith, trust, and love for themselves and others. I am calling these people Earth Angels who step up to change lives through **Love In Actions**.

Uniting modern day Harriet Tubmans, as Earth Angels in **Love In Actions**, is the heart of this journey.

The Underground Railroad was a movement guided by spirit and united in pursuit of freedom and dignity. Every action was powered by **Love In Actions**. I call this **Love In Actions** because love is not just a feeling; it is made real in our choices, steps, and words.

This little book, the first in a series of **Love In Actions** stories, was written to spark something in you. It's a reminder that love is not just a word to be spoken, but a way to live—and a legacy to leave.

In most chapters, I'll share a story from Harriet Tubman's life and another from my own experiences. I hope these stories help you discover your own way to share **Love In Actions** with your family, your friends, and the world.

Chapter Two

Planting Seeds of Self-Love and Unity

Sometimes, I think of self-love as a seed—something tiny but full of promise, waiting for the right time and care to bloom. In the Harriet Tubman **Love In Actions** Gift Box I share with others, I include a packet of flower seeds. I tell people these seeds already have everything needed to become the beautiful flowers they're meant to be; they just need to be planted and nourished. My life feels much the same. Looking back at my growth and my dreams for the future, I know God has prepared me to thrive. It just takes time, patience, and nourishment along the way.

Every day brings a new lesson—something that helps me add a little more nourishment to my spirit. As I keep learning about myself and the world, I grow stronger and more rooted in purpose.

When I first approached Rev. Terry about speaking at her church, she asked if I was familiar with Unity Church's teachings. I wasn't, so I started searching for answers. That's when I learned about Unity's Five Principles. To my surprise, these matched the ideas I already shared in my own books. Another meaningful coincidence—what I call a synchronicity.

Learning about Unity led me to wonder what other faiths had in common at their core. I began seeking out their simple, central teachings. The more I researched, the more I saw that—all differences aside—world religions share many of the same essential truths. Here is a simple guide to their wisdom:

Christianity

1. Faith in one God, known through Jesus Christ
2. Love God
3. Love your neighbor
4. Forgive others
5. Show compassion
6. Believe in eternal life through faith

Judaism

1. Believe in one God
2. Practice justice
3. Show mercy
4. Live honestly
5. Care for the community

Islam

1. Faith in one God (Allah)
2. Daily prayer

3. Giving to the poor
4. Fasting during Ramadan
5. Pilgrimage to Mecca

Mormonism (Latter-day Saints)

1. Faith in God, Jesus Christ, and the Holy Ghost
2. Accept Christ's atonement and follow through faith, repentance, and baptism
3. Value covenants and sacred ordinances
4. Trust both the Bible and Book of Mormon
5. Believe in ongoing guidance from living prophets
6. Focus on eternal family relationships
7. Health and mission service are important spiritual expressions

Hinduism

1. Dharma: Living with duty and purpose
2. Karma: Every action has consequences
3. Rebirth: Life continues in new forms
4. Moksha: Spiritual freedom and release

Buddhism

1. Right Understanding and Thought

2. Right Speech and Action

3. Right Livelihood, Effort, Mindfulness, and Concentration

4. The path is one of compassion and wisdom

Sikhism

1. Faith in one God

2. All people are equal

3. Serve others and live honestly

4. Dedicate life to God and the community

Indigenous and African Traditions

1. Deep connection to Creator, ancestors, and nature

2. Live in balance and respect all life

3. Honor the earth and keep strong community ties

4. See the sacred in all creation

Unity Church (Practical Christianity)

1. God is everywhere and always good

2. We are divine at our core

3. Our thoughts shape our lives

4. Prayer and meditation connect us with God

5. We live the truth by taking loving action

Centers for Spiritual Living (Science of Mind/CSL)

1. One Infinite Power and Presence
2. Our thoughts create our experience
3. Affirmative prayer brings healing and change
4. Love is the highest law
5. Abundance and oneness are for everyone

Spirituality (Interfaith/Personal)

1. Listen to inner guidance
2. Practice reflection or meditation
3. Honor many spiritual paths
4. Live with compassion, truth, and unity

Jehovah's Witnesses

1. Believe in one God, Jehovah
2. Accept Jesus as God's Son and Savior
3. Live by Bible standards
4. Remain politically neutral
5. Preach and share faith
6. Hope in God's Kingdom, with a focus on eternal life

Bahá'í Faith

1. The oneness of humanity
2. The oneness of all religions
3. Independent investigation of truth
4. Elimination of all forms of prejudice
5. Harmony of science and religion
6. Universal compulsory education
7. Equality of women and men
8. Universal auxiliary language
9. Abolition of extremes of wealth and poverty
10. Spiritual solution to economic problems
11. Establishment of universal peace
12. Work performed in the spirit of service is worship

Not one of these religious groups teach hate and fear of others.

Though the words, rituals, and customs are different, when you look past the surface, every tradition points back to the same eternal truths:

1. There is One Creator
2. Love and kindness are at the heart of everything

3. Forgiveness and healing are sacred

4. Helping others is a calling

5. Quiet time, prayer, or meditation keeps us connected

6. Honesty and fairness matter

7. Unity and connection are everyone's birthright

These shared values are the soil from which Harriet Tubman's faith grew. They're the same ground that supports my journey and gives me strength to tell my story.

Why does this matter?
Because when faith communities stand together in love, they help heal our world, set an example for society, and share hope wherever it's needed most. When we unite around what we share, we turn division into hope and create safe places where all people belong.

I feel God gave me an opportunity to break this cycle for the first announcement of this book, at a church where having two African Americans in the worship service, for the day—was truly divine intervention. It was an appropriate way to launch the New Underground Railroad. It's often said that the most segregated hour in America is Sunday morning. Even though our religions have so much in common, many worshippers still gather with those who look and think the same. If we believe in the same Creator, why aren't we praying, singing, and serving together?

This experience felt like a sacred calling to bridge divides, a reminder that real spiritual growth asks us to stretch beyond familiar boundaries. We each have a chance to challenge old patterns and foster unity—not just inside our churches, but everywhere we go. When we share stories and lift each other up, we honor God's vision of beloved community—a family that welcomes every voice, every gift, and every prayer. Perhaps the New Underground Railroad isn't only about freedom from physical chains, but about setting our hearts free to love beyond barriers, bringing people together in hope and harmony.

During Harriet Tubman's life, some churches broke these divisions—becoming active in the Underground Railroad and transforming into Safehouses for people fleeing to freedom. AME and AME Zion Churches, Quaker meeting houses, and Black congregations provided spiritual and real-world sanctuary. Today, the need is just as urgent. All faith communities must join in a new movement—opening doors, inviting diversity, and making true Safehouses of love.

My special group of people I am reaching out to are Grandmothers. We Grandmothers have the power to change lives. The number of women age 50 and older in the United States is remarkable, with approximately 44.7 million women in this age group as of 2025. Together, these women hold a combined financial strength exceeding $7 trillion dollars nationwide. Many have the gift of time, deep reserves of unconditional love, and generations of wisdom to share. This book is for everyone—for all ages and backgrounds—but I must honor the grandmothers, who possess a unique strength to bring **Love In Actions** to families, communities, and the world. The wisdom and love of grandmothers can heal generations.

It's no coincidence that cultures around the globe recognize the vital role of older women.

> The Hopi Native American tribe has a saying,
> "When grandmothers speak, the world will heal."

Grandmothers are often the hidden pillars who hold families together, pass down traditions, and call forth courage and compassion. As we lift up their voices and embrace their gifts, we help bring about the healing, unity, and transformative love our world needs.

As you journey through this book, you'll discover stories and reflections that invite you to notice the synchronicities in your own life—those moments when Spirit guides you toward love, unity, self-love, and deep compassion. Each chapter pairs a story from Harriet Tubman with one from my own experience, revealing how God's love and presence guide ordinary people in extraordinary ways. My hope is that these stories encourage you to find meaningful ways to put **Love In Actions** into practice—with your family, friends, and everyone whose path intersects with yours. This book is about awakening to the truth that divine timing, everyday miracles, and connections are available to all of us—if we pause to pay attention and respond with open hearts.

Lesson

At the heart of every faith is an invitation to love—love for ourselves, for others, and for the world. When we recognize our common ground, we gain the courage to move forward together. **Love In Actions** begins inside: by tending the seed of self-love and honoring our own spirit, we allow that goodness to overflow into compassion, unity, and healing for everyone we meet. In every tradition and every life, love is the nourishment that helps us grow strong, resilient, and free to serve.

Reflection Prompts

1. What does self-love mean to me, and how can I tend to it as I would nurture a seed?

2. Where have I noticed synchronicities—moments that felt divinely timed or meaningful—on my journey?

3. How do the core teachings of different faiths remind me of values I hold dear or experience in my own life?

4. In what ways can I help bridge divisions in my family, community, or place of worship?

5. What is one small act of love I can offer today to plant a seed for healing or connection?

6. How have grandmothers—whether in my family, community, or heritage—shared wisdom, resilience, or love that continues to shape my life? How can I honor or carry forward the healing power of grandmothers?

As you reflect on the stories, teachings, and seeds of love within these pages, remember that every life—especially the lives of grandmothers and elders—carries the power to heal, unify, and ignite new hope. May you cherish the synchronicities along your path, honor the wisdom handed down to you, and find your own unique ways to let **Love In Actions** flourish in your life and community. The journey to unity and self-love starts with a single step, and every small act of love truly matters.

Chapter Three

The New Underground Railroad

As we saw in Chapter two, every faith tradition calls us toward love, dignity, prayer, faith, action, and eternal hope. These shared truths are not just ideas; they are meant to be lived. Harriet Tubman's story shows us what happens when faith moves into action.

Harriet's Story

The Underground Railroad was not a train running on hidden tracks beneath the earth. It was people—Black, White, and Native American—who knew in their hearts that slavery was wrong. They chose courage over comfort, spirit over fear, and love over hate.

Harriet Tubman did not start the Underground Railroad. This movement began when the first enslaved people arrived in America and brave men and women sought freedom, while others chose to help them escape. By the time Harriet stepped into her role, the Railroad was already alive—an invisible yet powerful movement for freedom. Harriet's name became famous because her story was preserved in the book *Scenes in the Life of Harriet Tubman*, thanks to Sarah Bradford, who took the time to interview her and share her journey.

Harriet was born into slavery in Maryland around 1822. She faced harsh treatment, but her faith in God and her hope for freedom stayed strong. At age 25, Harriet's prayer and belief in her right to be free led her to take action:

"I had reasoned this out in my mind; there was one of two things I had a right to—liberty or death; if I could not have one, I would have the other, for no man should take me alive."

She escaped to Pennsylvania using the Underground Railroad—a secret network of people, safe houses, and hidden paths. She traveled by night, guided by the North Star, and relied on a chain of helpers along the way. Once free, Harriet didn't forget those left behind. Over the next decade, she risked her life on thirteen trips back to Maryland, helping about seventy enslaved people—including family and friends—find freedom.

Conductors like Harriet guided people north but depended on stationmasters—brave men and women who opened their homes, barns, and churches to provide food, shelter, and support. Together, they formed a living chain of courage stretching from the South to the free states in the North. Harriet became one of the most beloved and trusted conductors of all, known for her commitment and unshakable faith in God.

Harriet and the Five Unity Principles

As I learned about Unity's Five Principles, I saw them beautifully mirrored in Harriet's life:

She believed in a living God everywhere and in everyone. Her actions sprung from deep faith and a sense of her own worthiness and divine nature. She held tightly to hope and the power of possibility, even in the darkest circumstances. Prayer was her guide on every journey north, her lifeline in danger. Most of all, she lived her beliefs through loving, courageous action—risking everything so others might be free. I strive to live out these same truths—not just in my work, but in small, everyday ways. Harriet showed us that these spiritual ideas only matter when they move our hands, feet, and hearts.

My Story

My story with Harriet Tubman started when I worked at the Veterans Affairs Hospital in Tacoma, Washington. As chairperson for the African American Employees Equal Opportunity group, I taught about diversity and helped plan Black History Month programs. At the same time, I was learning storytelling at my Toastmasters Club.

In 1998, I watched Cicely Tyson play Harriet Tubman in *Harriet Tubman: The Moses of Her People*. Something about Harriet's courage moved me so much that I started researching her life and created a five-minute story for Toastmasters. That moment changed my life. For the past twenty-five years, I've shared Harriet's story with audiences and in my books, and have even been called "Harriet." I am proud to shine a light on her spirit, courage, and love.

Today, I feel called to share Harriet Tubman's stories as inspiration for all who recognize her as a compassionate and courageous leader. She was Black, poor, and illiterate, yet as worthy of dignity and respect as every person ever born. The Underground Railroad was the name given to a well-organized group of people who let love guide their actions. They didn't follow the written laws that said Harriet and her companions were property. Instead, they opened their hearts, homes, and wallets, following the voice within to help their sisters and brothers.

Now, I invite everyone to "Be Like Harriet"—to be brave, honest, and dedicated to helping others. Harriet was not just a leader; she was a servant leader, putting love into action one choice at a time. We may not be hiding fugitives in our homes, but we are called to open our hearts, voices, and resources to free others from the chains of hatred, poverty, violence, division, and despair. This is the New Underground Railroad.

Living the Call Today

Just as Harriet's time called for courage and unity, so does ours. We may not face slave catchers, but our communities still struggle with hatred in the streets, injustice in our systems, and painful divisions. And though the chains look different, slavery has not disappeared. Around the world, including here in the United States, millions remain trapped in human trafficking—bought, sold, and exploited for labor or sex. This $150 billion industry preys on the vulnerable, using fear and violence to keep people in bondage. Modern slavery also takes the form of addiction, poverty, or systemic oppression that strips people of dignity and opportunity.

This is where another synchronicity appeared in my life: I recently interviewed Ed Umoja Herman and his wife Dr. Kathleen Walls for my *GG United By Love Podcast*. Their mission is to educate and awaken people to the realities of human trafficking. Through their YouTube drama series *Kadaga*, they use storytelling to reveal the dangers and heartbreak of modern-day slavery. I had to share this with you—their work is a powerful way to raise awareness and motivate action.

Harriet's story reminds us: whenever people are held captive by chains, by fear, or by injustice, we are called to respond. Her legacy calls us to recognize all forms of bondage and to put our faith and love into action—right now, wherever we are.

The same Spirit that moved in Harriet calls us to act—to stand for freedom, practice unity, and turn our love into actions that heal, protect, and set others free.

Love In Actions Today

1. Learn the universal hand sign for help **(palm facing forward, thumb tucked in, then fingers closed over thumb)**. Share it so anyone in distress can signal for help.

2. Educate yourself about human trafficking locally and globally.

3. Support organizations that rescue survivors and provide safe housing, counseling, and skills for independence.

4. Use your voice to challenge systems of injustice, poverty, and exploitation.

5. Be a conductor—guide someone toward hope and freedom. Be a stationmaster—offer safe places and caring support. Be a supporter—use your gifts to make a difference.

6. Just as Harriet walked toward freedom, our call is to walk in solidarity with those still struggling—until all can live free.

Lesson

The Underground Railroad teaches us that freedom is not won by silence—it is won by faith and action. Love must move from words to deeds.

Reflection Prompts

1. What "chains" still enslave people in my community or the world today?

2. How can I listen for the "still, small voice" of Spirit guiding me to act?

3. What is one choice I can make this week that puts love into action?

4. What story or person from history inspires me to help others?

5. When have I put love into action, even in a small way?

6. What gift or strength can I use to help someone this week?

Harriet's journey reminds us: real change happens when ordinary people listen to their hearts, join together, and put love into action. Let us build a better world, one act of love, kindness, and courage at a time.

Chapter Four

Self-Love and Freedom

True Freedom Begins Within

In the last chapter, we explored the call to freedom for all people. But true freedom begins within. Harriet Tubman's story shows us that self-love was the foundation of her courage, and I later discovered it was also the foundation of my own.

Harriet's Story

Harriet Tubman was born Araminta "Minty" Ross in Maryland, the daughter of Benjamin Ross and Harriet "Rit" Green. Her parents were strong believers in God and taught Harriet to pray, hold onto hope, and trust that she was meant for freedom. Even from a young age, Harriet faced harsh treatment and hard work, but the spark of hope and faith always glowed in her heart.

She grew up deeply determined. When Minty set her mind to something, she held firm. While others lost faith or accepted their limits, Minty believed she was worthy of freedom. She listened to the quiet voice inside—the Holy Spirit—a voice that gave her strength to keep believing.

> "God's time is always near. He set the North Star in the heavens; He gave me the strength in my limbs; He meant I should be free."

Harriet didn't try to convince those who weren't ready. She helped those who wanted freedom enough to step into it. Guided by faith and self-love, Harriet fled slavery and risked her life to help others do the same. Her story is the Golden Rule lived out loud: Loving herself and honoring God's Spirit within let Harriet bless everyone she touched. For Harriet, **Love In Actions** meant seeing every person as worthy of dignity, joy, and peace—and acting to help them live free.

My Journey to Self-Love and Finding My Voice

For many years, I struggled to share my own story. Telling Harriet Tubman's story felt safe; her courage always inspired me. But opening up about my personal life was much harder—sometimes even frightening.

My marriage to James Brown was marked by privacy and silence. For forty-six years, I didn't speak about what was happening at home. Even our children were unaware of his chronic illness until 2014, when James was hospitalized for ten days—a long and stressful stretch that made his condition undeniable to the entire family. The following year, in 2015, James and I decided to leave Washington State and retire back to our hometown, Dayton, Ohio, hoping for peace near family. However, that sense of peace was short-lived. Forty-year old arguments resurfaced with greater intensity. In about year six of being back in Dayton, my 99-year-old mother moved in with us. The tension between James and me impacted her as well.

For six years, I lived as if I were captured. I left our home about six times, but always returned—held back by fear of change, fear of being alone, embarrassment, and shame.

Everything changed the night God spoke directly to me: "Get Out!" In that moment, I put fear behind me and asked for help—from Spirit, and from my family. A few weeks later, I left. Leaving marked the beginning of my own Underground Railroad.

As I drove away with my mother, a wave of relief washed over me. I was free. I finally understood what Harriet must have felt stepping into freedom—light, unburdened, hopeful. That moment later became the theme for my TEDx Oshawa 2024 talk, entitled: *The Freedom of Self-Love*. I shared in this speech how freedom felt light and beautiful, like a butterfly, and joy returned to me.

Leaving gave me the courage to write again. Before I left James, I'd tried many times to write a second edition of my book, "30 Lessons in Love, Leadership, and Legacy from Harriet Tubman," but the words wouldn't come. Only after I found my freedom did my true voice return, and the new book was born.

I have shared parts of my story in other book collaborations—one with Lisa Nichols, *"Rise Up! Ignite Your Inner Fire with Stories of Courage and Commitment,"* and another with Authors Who Care, *"Live a Positive Mindset, Love Can Make Anything Possible, Prosper."* Each time I told my story, it became a little easier. My journey to speak up about domestic violence grew into an important part of my TEDx topic and my deeper sense of purpose.

It was Zehra Mahoon—another Earth Angel on my path—who brought me into the Authors Who Care group and served as my coach for the TEDx Oshawa talk. I met Zehra through Lisa Nichols; just another example of how Spirit puts the right people in our lives when we're ready to take the next step. With Zehra's support, I truly found my voice as a woman called to help others act on self-love, joy, and freedom.

> Now my aim is to help women and girls everywhere understand that true self-love brings self-respect, empowerment, and confidence—reminding us that we are worthy and beautiful children of God.

This experience in my marriage became a vital piece in the puzzle of my life. As I write this book, more pieces—of every shape, size, and color—are finding their place, bringing clarity and new meaning to the picture of my life.

Lesson

True freedom begins with self-love—the courage to listen to Spirit's voice, honor your own needs, and step out of silence or fear. Like Harriet Tubman, and like my own journey, finding your voice is not selfish but sacred. When you choose self-love, you open the door to healing, purpose, and the ability to uplift others. Every act of loving yourself is a step toward the freedom God intended and a signal to others that lasting change is possible, one bold decision at a time.

Reflection Prompts

1. What hidden fears have kept me from sharing my story or asking for help?

2. Where in my life do I put others' feelings above my own safety or happiness?

3. What is one small act of self-love I can give myself today, even if I feel scared?

4. Who inspires me to show up bravely, and how could I reach out to support another person on their journey?

Self-love creates the courage for freedom. Let Harriet's and my stories invite you to listen for that inner voice, take the next brave step, and trust that healing and joy are possible for you too.

Chapter Five

Prayers and Connections

Prayer: A Lifeline to Spirit

"Once I began to love myself, I also began to rebuild my connection with God through prayer. Let's look at how Harriet relied on prayer and how it can become a lifeline for us too."

Harriet's Story

When Harriet Tubman was about fourteen, her life changed forever. She was not the target—a man running for his life was—but when the overseer threw a heavy weight, it struck Harriet in the head, knocking her unconscious. She was bedridden for months and, when she finally recovered, she was never quite the same.

After that injury, Harriet began experiencing headaches, fainting spells, and vivid dreams and visions. Sometimes they frightened her, but they also filled her with hope and pointed toward the future. Others saw these visions as a sign that God had a special plan for her life.

For nearly ten years, prayer was Harriet's constant companion. She prayed as she worked, as she washed her face, and as she sang spirituals in the fields. Prayer was her lifeline—her ongoing conversation with God. When she finally crossed into freedom at age twenty-five, the moment was so powerful that she said she had to look at her hands to see if she was still the same person. "It felt like I was in heaven."

But Harriet's story shows that prayer wasn't just for her escape. It sustained her through every season. Living in Auburn, New York, caring for family and friends, she sometimes wondered where the next meal would come from. There is a story about one of these occasions. There was no food, no money. Harriet went into her prayer closet and talked to God. When she came out, she told her sister-in-law, "Put a pot on the stove. We are going to have stew tonight." Then she'd walk into town, and the local vendors—who knew her well—filled her basket on credit. That night, the family ate together, with full bowls and grateful hearts.

Harriet's life teaches us that prayer is more than words. It is about trust, connection, and deep relationship with God. Prayer guided her through every trial and triumph, calling her into **love in Actions** over and over again. Prayer can do the same for us.

My Story

I grew up in the church, saying prayers before bed and meals. As I grew in spirit, I discovered that prayer is more than asking—it's about gratitude and affirming what God has already done. I learned to trust that I have everything I need because I am cared for by God.

Around 2022, after my mother and I moved into our own apartment, I rewatched the movie The Secret, which is all about the law of attraction. My mother, Frances Moss Moore, was 100 years old then—still sweet and loving, but with some short-term memory challenges. After we watched the movie, I asked her what she thought. She said it was okay, but she didn't really believe it.

I told her, "I do believe it." I pointed to how my children set goals and accomplished them as living proof of the movie's message. To help my mother see a new perspective, we watched The Secret again and again, at least twenty times. For her, every viewing was new. For me, the ideas started to sink in and become part of who I am.

That interest led me to follow teachers from the film, especially Lisa Nichols, Rev. Michael Beckwith, Bob Proctor, Mike Dooley, and Neale Donald Walsch. Some more synchronicities showed up along the way: My daughter, Atiara, is a Certified Self-development Coach for the Proctor Gallagher Institute (Bob Proctor's organization), and she coached me with the program Thinking Into Results, Program for Leaders. This experience deepened my commitment to my faith and strengthened my belief that God has put this book in my heart for a reason. I am being guided by my thoughts to have my programs make a difference in lives of others. To be of service. Another puzzle piece fell into place.

Through their messages, I learned to develop daily practices of prayer, meditation, and something called automatic writing—writing down whatever comes to you when you ask Spirit a question and let the answers flow freely. This has become how I begin each day, connecting me more deeply to God and to myself.

As I followed this path, my beliefs became less about the rules I learned in the religious teachings before this time, and more in line with the Unity Church:

Oneness with God, love as a guiding principle, and believing in abundance for all.

I now see self-love and my connection to God as the roots of every blessing in my life—a theme I explore in The Harriet Tubman Way book.

Now, my prayers are no longer about just asking for God to do things, fix the world, change people. They are about affirmation, declaring what I believe is already true and trusting God's presence in every moment of my life. I see affirmative prayer as an active way of practicing faith—a form of gratitude, saying "thank you" to God for what has already been done. It's like the seeds of love and gifts planted within each of us; when we nurture and grow them, we discover that we already have everything we need inside to become who we are meant to be, and to receive what we are truly worthy of. Here is an example of an affirmative prayer.

Affirmative Prayer

I am free to love myself
The Spirit of God lives within me
Divine wisdom guides me
Infinite love surrounds me
I am not alone. I am not forgotten.
I release fear, shame, and judgment
I forgive myself and others
I step forward with courage,
listening to the voice of love within me
I am worthy of love. I am guided by grace
I am free to be all I came here to be
And so it is, Amen

Affirmative prayer starts my day with gratitude, hope, and trust. It helps me stay open to feel the Spirit of God and show up as my true self, ready for loving action.

Lesson

Prayer is not just asking; it's affirming God's presence, power, and love in our lives. When we pray in this way, our trust in God grows, our fears fade, and we are moved to loving action that blesses others, too.

Reflection Prompts

1. Do I see prayer only as asking, or do I also use it to affirm God's blessings in my life?

2. How can I deepen my practice of prayer so it becomes a steady lifeline of trust, courage, and love in action?

3. How often do I talk to God?

4. What is one way I can make prayer more a part of my daily life?

Prayer is a gift that connects us to God, grounds us in self-love, and helps us take loving action, one day at a time.

Chapter Six

Faith and Foresight

Faith and Foresight: Trust in Action

Prayer leads us to trust God's voice, but it also requires us to act with courage. In this chapter, see how Harriet's faith and foresight worked together to guide her, and how they can guide us.

What is Foresight, Spiritually?

Foresight is more than seeing ahead with the mind; it's a spiritual openness that listens for God's guidance, trusting that God not only leads but prepares the way. In this book, foresight means blending faith with insight—trusting your inner voice but also planning and acting with intention. It's the heart listening to God's Spirit's whispers while the hands move with wisdom and hope for what's possible.

Harriet's Story

As a conductor on the Underground Railroad, Harriet Tubman was more than a traveler; she was a guide and leader, responsible for bringing others from slavery to freedom. She used everything she had: her knowledge of the woods, the stars, and the wisdom of her mother, father, and grandmother. Faith made her brave. Foresight made her wise.

Harriet planned her trips carefully, using the North Star as her compass. She walked softly through winter's woods, traveling at night, reading the signs of nature. Winter, though bitter, provided longer, darker nights and fewer people outside—making it easier to, as the song says, "steal away."

That wisdom, mixed with faith, is why Harriet made about thirteen trips, guiding some seventy people to freedom—and never lost a single passenger. She once said,

"I was the conductor of the Underground Railroad for eight years, and I can say what most conductors can't say, I never ran my train off the track, and I never lost a passenger."

One winter night, Harriet traveled north with three men. The snow crunched under their feet, and frozen air numbed their hands and faces. Suddenly, Harriet's heart began to pound—a sign she believed was God's warning. She turned to the men and said, "Brothers, we must get off this road."

They trusted her, leaving the familiar path for the woods. Soon, they reached a stream rimmed with ice, with no way around it. Harriet stepped into the bone-chilling water first, wading across. Halfway through, she whispered,

> "Oh Lord, you've been with me through six troubles.
> Do not leave me in the seventh."

The men followed once they saw she had made it safely.

Exhausted but unharmed, they continued on. God led them to a small cabin deep in the woods. Kind people welcomed the group, offered food, dried their clothes, and gave them a safe place to sleep.

The next day, Harriet learned patrols were waiting on the road ahead. Her obedience to God's prompting and careful planning had saved every life.

Faith and foresight walked hand in hand for Harriet. She trusted God's voice and used wisdom to plan her steps; her "train never jumped a track," and kindness carried her and her passengers safely onward.

My Story: The Vision—A Chain Reaction of Love

I want to invite readers to look at the possibilities of **Love In Actions**. God's spirit has shown me a vision:

Imagine a world where **Love In Actions** sparks like dominoes, each touch passing on the energy of kindness and wisdom. The domino effect is a chain reaction where one action sets off a sequence of related events, like a row of dominoes falling—each one triggering the next in line. It begins with grandmothers who choose self-love and accept God's plan for their lives. These women share their stories of struggle, triumph, and how God brought them through it all. Their personal journeys become wisdom—wisdom that is meant to be shared. This wisdom and the natural unconditional love that grandmothers are known for is a gift to their families—a gift that comes from God.

In the spirit of God's teachings, family is meant to be our sacred circle—a shelter for growth, resilience, and encouragement, where unconditional love is modeled and passed down. As grandmothers pour love, faith, and wisdom into their families, the ripple spreads to children and grandchildren, igniting compassion, courage, and unity as God's children. Through every act of nurture and spiritual guidance, grandmothers help build the spiritual foundation that heals, strengthens, and transforms families and communities across generations.

I see the grandmothers as the first domino to connect to others, and to impact all those coming after them.

If every home lived like this, we would soon see a world transformed—fear and hatred melt away, replaced by peace, harmony, and true happiness.

The synchronicities continue. As I study A Course In Miracles (ACIM) daily, I find practical wisdom for living guided by God. ACIM is a spiritual self-study program designed to guide people toward love, forgiveness, and inner peace. Its teachings help us shift from fear to love, emphasizing spiritual transformation through forgiveness and inspired action. ACIM offers a framework for living by spiritual guidance, aligning our thoughts and choices with God's divine love.

I follow the daily guide and I find that each lesson arrives exactly when I need it. Engaging with these lessons affirms my purpose—another synchronicity in my journey. There are 365 lessons in ACIM. I didn't start at the beginning of the year, but when I started writing this book, I was at:

Lesson 95: "I Am One Self, United with My Creator."

This lesson was the first to specify practice sessions for the first five minutes of each hour. This structure reminded me to "Be like Harriet," praying all day and staying connected to God every moment.

It sounds simple to pray every hour, but building new habits takes time. I started by drinking more water, and every time I go to the bathroom, I say an affirmative prayer, a word of gratitude. I am still working toward every hour.

Joy and happiness are what I consider living with self-love.

ACIM teaches that happiness is not a distant hope, but God's true will for each of us.

These lessons say joy is rooted in spiritual truth—a sign that we are aligned with God's love and purpose. To live joyfully is to honor God within, and to let self-love radiate out, blessing our families, communities, and the world.

More lessons from A Course in Miracles (ACIM) ACIM Student Workbook

> Lesson 98: "I will accept my part in God's plan for salvation."

This means each person has a vital role in bringing love, healing, and kindness into the world. God's plan works through us—we are each **Love In Actions**. Saying yes to this part lets our lives bless others.

> Lesson 101 teaches: "God's will for me is perfect happiness."

This invites us to believe that joy and peace are not far-off dreams. God's hope for us is available right now. I have learned that when we are living with love, wisdom, and courage, following examples like Harriet and wise grandmothers, we are helping God. Self-love is how we help fulfill God's purpose for us. Self-love leads to a life full of happiness—happiness that will expand out into our families, communities, nations, and the world.

Lesson

Foresight is faith in motion. When we blend prayer, practical planning, and trust, we see beyond problems and step into the new possibilities God prepares. Like Harriet, and in my journey, we are called to listen, trust, and act—even when the way is uncertain. As Alexandra, from the DIVA Network, teaches us to *Show Up Scared*.

Reflection Prompts

1. When has my inner voice nudged me to choose a different path? Did I listen?

2. How might my life change if I trusted and acted on those nudges with courage, like Harriet?

3. What is one step of planning or preparation I can take today that shows my faith in action?

4. Where do I need to blend both faith and foresight, so I'm not stuck in one place?

5. How can I help spark **Love In Actions** in my own life, family, or community?

Affirmation

For Harriet Tubman Day in 2024, my theme was "I Am Harriet Tubman." I created t-shirts, mugs, a red and black tote bag with Harriet's portrait, painted by my daughter, Adia, with the words:

I Am Harriet Tubman. Take a moment after repeating these words to feel the power behind them.

I invite you to say this affirmation three times and let it become part of your spirit:

I Am Harriet Tubman

I Am Harriet Tubman

I Am Harriet Tubman

This is more than a name—It's a legacy of Faith, Foresight, Courage, and **Love In Actions**. I carry Harriet's spirit every time I choose love and faith and I step forward to help or heal. And so it is. Amen.

Chapter Seven

Love in Actions: Faith That Moves

Every journey of faith brings new opportunities—and new challenges—to step out in courage. As we move deeper into the legacy of Harriet Tubman, we not only reflect on her powerful stories, but also find ways to draw strength from her example and those guiding voices within our own lives. This chapter invites you to discover how faith, action, and the leadership of family can transform personal history into a legacy of hope. Building on our understanding of faith and foresight, this chapter explores how stepping into action shapes our lives and our communities.

Harriet's Story

Harriet's faith was never something she kept private or quiet. Her trust in God was lived out in every action she took, and she depended on God's protection and direction at every step. At the same time, she used the mind and gifts God gave her—resourcefulness, quick thinking, and courage—especially when danger was close.

Most people know about her daring journeys on the Underground Railroad and her service with the Union Army. But Harriet's willingness to step into action did not end there. Even in the so-called "free" states, she kept on fighting for justice wherever she found injustice. One powerful example took place in Troy, New York. By then, slavery had been abolished in New York, but the Fugitive Slave Law meant anyone who had escaped bondage could still be captured and sent back—even in the North. That's why Harriet often guided people all the way to Canada, where the laws of slavery could not reach.

In Troy, a man named Charles Nalle was about to be sent back to slavery, betrayed even by his own half-brother. Looking at the two men, you might not even tell them apart, but because Charles's mother was Black, the law said he was Black too. And being Black meant he could be enslaved. This case tragically showed there was more than one way that slavery could divide families, and how, under the law, a person's fate depended on ancestry and color. When word spread that Harriet Tubman had arrived, she and the local community stood united, refusing to let Charles be taken. The rescue that followed was dramatic, more like a riot in the streets than a quiet escape. Black and white townspeople risked their own safety to pull Charles from the hands of those who claimed him. At the center was Harriet Tubman, willing once again to step up and step out for what was right.

> This reminds me of Congressman John Lewis's "Good Trouble." “Good Trouble” means making necessary, peaceful trouble to stand up against injustice and create meaningful social change—even if it means challenging unfair laws or systems.

Harriet never doubted that God was with her. She believed that when she acted from love, she could not fail. That was her superpower: **Love In Actions**. Living faith, for Harriet, meant doing more than believing in God's promises. It meant having the courage to act on them, no matter the risk.

My Act of Faith: The Stepping Stone Journey

Harriet's faith and foresight taught me to use my own gifts of leadership, my sense of responsibility for others, and my passion to lead the way to freedom—not always freedom of the body, but freedom of the conscience.

Just as Harriet stopped in her tracks in obedience to God's voice, I depend on God speaking through my intuition—those gut feelings, those inner insights shaped by hindsight and wisdom. When God whispers "It's Time to Go!", I have learned to listen. If you ignore that voice, you may find yourself stuck in a kind of slavery—bound by fear, doubt, or regret.

This is why I am telling my story. Because I listened to God. In my faith and foresight, I am Harriet Tubman—trusting, following, and leading with courage. *Keep the Spirit of A Leader* is the first chapter in *30 Lessons in Love, Leadership and Legacy from Harriet Tubman*. I have been teaching this lesson for many years. Now I know why. Because this is my message that I have come to share with the world.

Writing this book and starting the GG United by Love Podcast have been acts of living faith for me. When I first felt called to bring grandmothers together in a united movement, I trusted the vision that God placed on my heart even before I could see where each step might lead. Sharing this purpose began to draw "Earth Angels"—spiritual guides and encouragers—into my life: people whose words or actions inspired chapters in this book, offered

encouragement, or introduced new causes to address. Each connection strengthened my calling and reminded me to let God guide my heart.

I suggest you look back from where you are and see if you can call the names of some "Earth Angels"—the special people whose influence or encouragement made a difference. There are many I can name, but I am focusing on this book and those who I can connect directly to this project. However, I do want to add that as soon as I started watching "The Secret" and following Lisa Nichols, more of these special people have been drawn to me. One is Melanie Soloway, whom I met through Lisa, and through Melanie, I met Alexandra Silva Labarr, whose book motivated me to *Show Up Scared*.

I've come to believe everyone has a unique calling and something special to contribute to the world. In many African traditions, it is said,

> "It takes a village to raise a child."

The truth is, the village begins at home—with the elders, the parents, and all the generations that came before, surrounding each child with love, wisdom, and guidance. When the full family—grandmothers, grandfathers, mothers, fathers, aunts, uncles, cousins—work together, every child has a much stronger foundation to grow and thrive.

My own journey often feels like crossing a river on stepping stones—a path set by God long before I started walking it. Some stones are sturdy and clear, leading directly toward purpose. Others are slippery; sometimes I fall or need to double back and start again. Sometimes the path meandered through a maze or leads into deep water, and I have to pause, refocus, and move forward with help from those traveling with me.

Each new beginning, and each lesson learned from family and community, deepens my wisdom. Just like "a domino effect", every small action or connection can set off a chain reaction of love, support, and transformation that touches many lives.

Over time, every step—every success and every slip—has shaped who I am. When we persevere and lean on our family and spiritual "village," the next steps become clearer, and the journey gets easier. Eventually, our path is familiar enough that we can guide others across too, multiplying the number of people who reach their purpose with confidence and fewer missteps.

Our children need guidance from wise people. Having loving, wise grandparents—or "community grandparents"—in their lives becomes a defining factor in how children learn to live as caring, compassionate citizens. This multigenerational support helps instill values, resilience, and emotional intelligence. It is through these rooted relationships that we change society: nurturing future generations to lead with empathy, kindness, and shared purpose.

Lesson

Families are the sacred soil where our faith is nourished and made real. When we put faith into action with and for our loved ones—caring, teaching, forgiving, and serving together—we build a foundation strong enough to weather any challenge. Harriet's story reminds us that the greatest acts of justice and love begin at home, within a circle of trust and support. By living **Love In Actions** as a family, our collective faith becomes unstoppable, planting seeds of hope that flourish across generations.

Reflection Prompts

As you meditate on Harriet's story and your own journey, consider these reflections:

1. What is one "stepping stone" moment in my life—a time when I learned from a setback or a new beginning?

2. Who are the "Earth Angels" I've encountered, and how did their words or actions encourage me to keep moving forward?

3. In what ways have I helped someone else on their journey,

sharing wisdom from my own experience?

4. What is one small action I can take today to start, or continue, my journey of living purpose and **Love In Actions**?

5. How might my story help multiply love and confidence in others as they seek their own purpose?

6. How has my family—whether birth, chosen, or spiritual—helped shape my journey of faith, resilience, and love?

7. In what ways can I strengthen those bonds or offer support, guidance, or wisdom to my loved ones today?

Let Harriet's story and mine inspire you to listen, to trust, and to step forward in love, turning faith into action—and your actions into a legacy that will brighten the path for others.

Chapter Eight

Love and Compassion in Action

In the last chapter, we explored how faith truly comes alive through living faith in actions—how Harriet Tubman trusted God and boldly stepped out, letting her faith speak through acts of courage and commitment. Now we turn to the source of motivation behind those brave choices: Love and Compassion.

Harriet's Story

For 25 years, I have portrayed Harriet Tubman. Stepping into her story, I often asked myself: Why did she go back? Why risk her life again and again for others?

During the pandemic, I recorded my Harriet stories with students and staff at Wright State University in Dayton, Ohio. Out of that experience came my film, "Harriet Tubman: Love in Action." Later, I realized it should have been called "**Love In Actions**," because real love always multiplies.

In the film, Harriet is asked, "Why did you go back?" One word captures her answer: Love. It was love that drove Harriet—love for her family and love for her people. She grew up immersed in a strong sense of community among the enslaved, a chosen family who sustained one another in the darkest times. Women were Sister, Auntie, Mama, Big Mama. Men were Brother, Uncle. Her father, Ben Ross, was known as "Daddy Ben" to all the children. That nurturing community, built on compassion, kept everyone going.

When Harriet first escaped, she left behind her husband, John Tubman, who was legally free but still deeply vulnerable. She fled with the hope of returning for him, but learned he had chosen a new wife. Harriet's heartbreak did not make her bitter—it grew her compassion. She turned her love toward those ready and willing to risk everything for freedom.

Harriet knew love must move.

> Frederick Douglass said, "I prayed for freedom for 25 years but received no answer until I prayed with my legs."

Harriet could have stayed in the safety of the North, simply praying for her loved ones from afar. But compassion stirred her to act. She made the journey back 13 times, risking everything so all she could reach would taste freedom.

Her life was a living testimony to love that risks, love that acts, love that serves.

My Story

Portraying Harriet has changed me and continues to do so. My days are filled with creating workshops, books, stories, podcasts, and events for people I may never meet. Sometimes I question if my family fully sees these acts as love, or if they see it as just the way I am—always busy. But the truth is, bringing people together, organizing health events, Harriet Tubman Day, International Day of the Girl Child, Grandparents Day—this has always been my way of expressing love and compassion.

What truly nourishes me is the love in my heart that yearns to bring joy to others. When a program I create delights someone, when a message resonates, or a story opens a heart, I feel joy too. My podcast brings out stories from women who say they don't have anything to share—"I am just me, an average person." I help them realize they are gifts from God with their own action to take. I am here to help others see their worth, feel loved, and shine.

It is no coincidence that this book is launching at a Unity Church during a month themed "Synchronicities and Serendipities." Rev. Terry's teaching from Eric Butterworth's "In the Flow of Life" feels like an affirmation. In chapter eight of this book, Butterworth writes, "You don't grow old. When you stop growing, you are old." He also teaches, "The wisdom of the world has conditioned us to 'act our age.' Now we must begin to act our youth, to act our experience in the flow of life."

You have heard people say, "Today is the first day of the rest of our lives"—because it truly is. If you wake up, you are still here to feel the joy of life. Joy, love, happiness—they have no age limit. So, grandmothers and grandfathers, let's have some fun! Be the spark at family parties.

Share your stories and laughter. Teach young people how to mature gracefully and how to live life out loud.

Living life "out loud" means being true to your authentic self—showing your real feelings, values, dreams, and gifts to the world, instead of hiding or shrinking in the background because we think we are "too old".

It's living on purpose: expressing love, standing up for what matters to you, sharing your story, and allowing your light to be seen and heard, no matter what others might think.

An everyday act of love in my life is my morning quiet time—a sacred pause that anchors my soul. If I don't start my day with prayer and meditation, then I make sure to end it that way. This is how I practice self-love: appreciating that I am blessed in the only moment in time that matters—now.

Live from the inside out. Even on the slippery stones, God is still holding our hands.

Lesson

Love and compassion must move us into action—choices that may stretch us, but bring hope, freedom, and belonging to others and ourselves.

Reflection Prompts

1. Where in my life do I need to move love from words into actions?

2. What would it look like for me to "pray with my feet" today?

3. Who in my life needs not just my prayers, but my actual support or presence?

4. How can I make love the core motivation behind my choices this week?

5. What acts of love do I offer, whether noticed or unseen, that bring me joy and meaning?

6. How does the idea of "growing onward" inspire my next step?

Let Harriet's story, this book, and your own journey call you into deeper love and compassion. Be willing to act, to serve, and to shine your light—knowing that by giving, you grow onward, not old, and are always held in God's loving hand.

Chapter Nine

Eternal Life and Legacy

Legacy of Love: Generations in Motion

"Faith in action" is not just a single moment—it ripples through generations. Harriet Tubman's roots, her visions, and her grandmother's stories became a legacy of freedom. In this chapter, I reflect on how these legacies, and my own, carry love forward.

Harriet's Story

Harriet Tubman inherited deep spiritual roots. Her father, Ben Ross, was a man of faith and vision—what we would now call an herbalist or mystic. He understood plant medicine, how to read the woods, and how to listen to God's creation. Harriet carried the same gifts. She sometimes saw things before they happened.

Before the Civil War, while staying with a friend, she danced and sang, "My people are free! My people are free!" Some doubted, saying, "Freedom will come, but not in our lifetime." Harriet was happy; she trusted it was God showing her the truth. She was celebrating because she had already seen freedom.

She dreamed of John Brown's death before it happened. She held the vision of freedom before others dared hope. Her spiritual sight gave her both courage and urgency to act.

Her grandmother Modesty was said to have been born in Africa. I imagine her sharing stories of their ancestors—kings, queens, and families who lived free and in peace, joy and unity before slavery. These stories weren't just comfort; they were legacy. They taught Harriet and her family that dignity, freedom, and greatness lived in their blood, no matter what the world said.

It's possible Modesty remembered how, in Africa, unity and community were ways of life. These truths echo in the Seven Principles of Kwanzaa, which align beautifully with the spiritual foundation of this book and point back to universal truths:

Umoja (Unity): Oneness with God and each other.
Kujichagulia (Self-Determination): Self-love and identity.
Ujima (Collective Work and Responsibility): **Love In Actions**.
Ujamaa (Cooperative Economics): Sharing and service.
Nia (Purpose): Divine calling and foresight.
Kuumba (Creativity): Prayer and creative expression.
Imani (Faith): The heart of living faith in actions.

Legacy is **Love In Actions**. Harriet Tubman told her stories to everyone. She became a professional storyteller and activist for the abolitionist movement, using her voice to inspire and raise funds to return and rescue others. Her stories were so powerful that Sarah Bradford felt compelled to write a book about her. Bradford not only documented Harriet's life for all of us, but also helped Harriet save her home by selling the book and enabling her to pay her mortgage. Recording and sharing these stories about Harriet Tubman has blessed, inspired, and amazed generations. What a legend. This is how sharing stories is a living example of **Love In Actions**.

My Story

Legacy lives in us. Love never dies—it connects us to our ancestors, and to our children and grandchildren. Through love, we honor those who came before us and ensure their wisdom and spirits live on within us. Love is the invisible thread binding generations together—offering strength, courage, and belonging, no matter how much time has passed.

My maternal grandmother was Nancy L. Webster. She lived to be 101. She insisted her ten grandchildren attend Sunday School and Baptist Training Union (BTU). We learned Bible verses and recited poems. She taught me how to make handmade corsages for Mother's Day. I was the only one who learned, and floral design is still my hobby. Grandmother started a flower business and shared her love freely, becoming “Grandmother” to everyone in our neighborhood.

My mother was Frances Moss Moore. She also lived to be 101. She was an author and actress who made her first TV commercial at age 75. She was active in Toastmasters and volunteered at the Paul Laurence Dunbar home, dressing in early 1900s fashion while reciting poems. She organized programs and fundraisers for the church and wrote a book about my grandmother’s life. These stories offer family sayings, jokes, and heartwarming memories that would have been lost if she hadn’t recorded them. Through stories, we have a legacy that lives on. As they say, “The apple doesn’t fall far from the tree.”

If you read my resume, you’ll find I’ve been part of the Love of Dunbar, a group of people who come together to recite Paul Laurence Dunbar’s poems. I plan to make a commercial before I turn 75. (Smile)

My sister, Joyce A. Barnes, is an educator, author, and has founded a nonprofit program called The Economic Emancipation Monetary Fund, or "A Dollar A Month" program. Joyce is teaching us how each of the ten million of African American families in the United States—if each family contributed $1.00 a month—that would be the beginning of an endowment to support our community’s freedom from all the forms of bondage we now suffer. This is an example of the New Underground Railroad, which represents modern efforts for community empowerment and support. This program is bringing financial literacy and financial benefits to the Black community. It also shows how we both learned community from our mother and grandmother.

From Nancy L. Webster and Frances Moss Moore, we inherited not just long lives, but a living example of **Love In Actions**. They showed me we are all strong, creative, courageous, and loving—and called to carry that forward.

Just as Harriet drew strength from her grandmother, and as I did from both my grandmother and mother, today our grandchildren need our strength and our nonjudgmental, unconditional love. The stories, faith, and actions we share become their foundation. Let's give them the gift of our love and wisdom to carry forward.

The Seven Principles of Kwanzaa have nothing to do with religion. Kwanzaa is a week-long celebration of African American culture, held from December 26 to January 1 every year. Families light candles on a kinara, discuss the principle for each day, share stories, enjoy special meals, and celebrate with music, dance, and gifts that honor heritage. Kwanzaa offers an ideal opportunity to teach our children about love and the responsibility of family and community. Earlier this year, my cousin Kathy Banks, taught me that the Kwanzaa ceremony of lighting candles doesn't have to be used only at the end of December. It can and should be shared and encouraged anytime. This inspired me to have a Kwanzaa celebration during my recent wedding ceremony. It was a special way of uniting two families.

The Seven Principles of Kwanzaa: Passing On the Legacy of Love

The Seven Principles of Kwanzaa (Nguzo Saba) are not only for African Americans, but echo universal values that connect us to our ancestors and help us build loving, rooted homes and communities. These principles are a guide for teaching and practicing

Love In Actions, just as Harriet, Modesty, Nancy, Frances, and so many others—unknown and unnamed—have done.

How to Use the Principles at Home

Introduce each principle by name and meaning. Use stories—whether from Harriet, Modesty, Nancy, Frances, or your own family—to show how every principle lives on in your history. Invite loved ones to reflect and share:

Umoja (Unity): How do we practice unity as a family? Where have we shown oneness or togetherness?

Kujichagulia (Self-Determination): What traditions help us honor our identity or set our own paths?

Ujima (Collective Work and Responsibility): When have we worked together or looked out for each other?

Ujamaa (Cooperative Economics): How do we share resources and support one another?

Nia (Purpose): What dreams or goals have been passed down in our family?

Kuumba (Creativity): What special ways do we express love, solve problems, or create joy?

Imani (Faith): In which moments have we kept faith—whether in each other, God, or a brighter future?

Encourage each family member, especially children and grandchildren, to connect stories, photos, or memories to each principle. This practice creates a living family “Legacy of Love Journal.”

Activity: Create a Family Legacy of Love Journal

Get a blank journal.

Label a section or page for each principle.

Invite family members to add a story, drawing, or photo:

- A memory about an ancestor that connects to the principle.
- How the family is practicing the principle now.
- Hopes, prayers, or intentions for the future.
- Review the journal as a family—during Kwanzaa, reunions, or birthdays.

This tradition will help everyone share wisdom and belonging, and celebrate the power of love over generations.

Lesson

Legacy is eternal love in motion. Our bodies may pass away, but the spirit of love, wisdom, and courage never dies. Stories, prayers, and **Love In Actions** can shape generations. Legacy is not just history—it lives in us, and it is ours to pass on.

Reflection Prompts

1. What wisdom, story, or prayer from my ancestors still lives within me?
2. How can I share my own story of love and strength, so my children and grandchildren carry it forward?
3. What "love in actions" do I want to be remembered for when

future generations call my name?

4. Who in your family carries the spirit of Umoja—holding the family together in hard times?

5. Which family stories fill you with pride and purpose? How can you record or retell them for the next generation?

6. What new traditions could honor these principles and grow your family's legacy of love?

Let this chapter be your invitation to remember, record, and renew the legacy of self-love, faith in action, and joyous community stretching from Harriet Tubman to your own family, its blessings rippling into generations yet to come.

Chapter Ten

Love In Actions

When Courage Calls

"**Love In Actions**" isn't about a single leap—it's the faith to believe, the courage to move, the trust that freedom is possible, and the resolve to nurture healing for both self and others.

Harriet's Story

When Harriet Tubman was about 25, the threat of being sold away to the "Deep South" loomed over her and two of her brothers. Her family had already endured heartbreak—three of her sisters had been sold, never seen again. Harriet resolved not to let this happen to her.

She first attempted escape with her brothers, but fear caused them to turn back. Still, Harriet's spirit could not surrender to captivity. Not long after, she left again—this time alone—and pressed forward until she crossed into freedom. Later, she described the moment:

> "It felt so glorious, I had to look at my hands to see if I was the same person."

For Harriet, freedom was something felt both physically and spiritually—"like heaven come to earth."

My Story

As described in earlier chapters, my path to self-liberation and healing included overcoming fear, letting go of what no longer served me, and learning that every brave act of leaving is also a journey toward reclaiming joy.

This chapter is about my journey and the synchronicities that brought me to write this book.

Our first daughter, Adia, is named from Swahili and means "A Gift from God." Adia was born on November 12, 1974, I remeber the nurse telling me I had a beautiful little girl with dimples. Years later, I would have a Harriet Tubman Love In Actions Gift Box, and now I call it my Adia Gift Box to honor my daughter.

Ariessunna is our son, named by his father. He chose the name because he was the son of an Aries, and wanted double letters for strength, and to show the connection to the sun. Our youngest daughter, Atiara, is my crown and my jewel.

In 1987, our family's move from Dayton, Ohio to Seattle, Washington, tested our resilience. We moved on nothing but faith and $5,000. We knew nobody and had no jobs. (Young and brave—or as some said, stupid! LOL!) God was with us. He sent help when we needed it. There was unexpected kindness—like the lady, a stranger in Iowa, who helped when our car broke down on the second day of our journey. It was a Friday, and the repair would not be finished until Monday. This lady drove our family to a hotel in a great location for entertaining the children and shopping for our needs. This was a demonstration of how **Love In Actions** paves the way when you trust God.

We built new lives in Washington. My career led me to the Veterans Affairs Hospital and to creating my first Harriet Tubman storytelling program. I chose to portray Harriet as an elderly woman—"Aunt Harriet." This version of Harriet was known as the woman who loved people, opened her home to the homeless, and donated property to her church, the African Methodist Zion, (AME Zion Church), which built the Harriet Tubman Home for the Elderly in Auburn, New York. She made this contributions of 25 acres she purchased at auction, when she was in her eighties. Although she had no money upfront. Harriet secured a loan by putting up the property as collateral. This is the Harriet Tubman most people don't know—the "Community Grandmother," Aunt Harriet.

That's why I was able to play Harriet in my forties. I used what is rooted in family tradition, blending my grandmother Nancy Webster's voice, sayings, and wisdom with Harriet's strength. Becoming Harriet Tubman was a major stepping stone in my life. Her stories became part of my legacy, shaping how I would later encourage others to reclaim their purpose and joy.

The biggest changes came later, and they were unexpected. Our marriage was altered by illness and mental health challenges. God spoke to me through a quiet spiritual nudge, pushing me to finally say, "Get out!" That act of leaving—guided by intuition and faith—became my own moment of crossing into freedom.

Years before, I had started meditating, which helped me. I drew strength from journaling. My meditation practice was inspired by Oprah and Deepak Chopra. Gradually, it helped me rebuild the foundation of my life. Grief support and family encouragement gave me the peace and joy that motivated me to write *The Harriet Tubman Way* book. What began as a study in servant leadership was refined by necessity when I shifted to teaching self-love—a message I had to learn first, for myself.

I learned about "energy vampires"—people who, sometimes unknowingly, drain others' spirit and energy—through personal experience. I realized that was the relationship I was living in for longer than eight years. It was not all bad, but it was not free. My friend Brenda McKinney, a minister and longtime mental health counselor, said to me,

"Sometimes you don't know you are a prisoner until you get free." That recognition became part of my healing and motivated me to support others, especially women and teenage girls dealing with similar struggles.

While in Dayton, I supported my family, maintained our house, and an apartment with my mother. I relied on God's provision for what I needed. When it was time to get rid of my 20-year-old car and needed a job, I found the perfect job in just one day. I got my car and started teaching at an after school program.

That's when I realized how important it is to teach our children to love themselves. I know we become what we say to ourselves, so it hurt me to hear one young girl say every day, "I'm stupid." Unfortunately, she had to leave the afterschool program to care for her two younger brothers. I especially saddened for her, after her grandmother—the glue who kept the family together—passed away. I knew my mission was to help our girls, as they become women, learn how to love themselves.

The unique details of my journey—new cities, new challenges, learning to accept help, and practicing daily gratitude—taught me that every choice, connection, and even setback, is for a reason. When I share my stories of how I have grown on this journey, is like dropping breadcrumbs of hope for someone else to follow. Also, every act of kindness, every change in direction, is another way of leaving breadcrumb pointing the way toward healing.

Lesson

Finding freedom and healing isn't sudden—it's the result of many small acts: choosing courage over fear, practicing self-love, and turning struggle into new purpose. The more we listen, love, and let our stories grow, the more we clear a path that others can follow.

Reflection Prompts

1. What steps, moves, or names have shaped my journey and the meaning I carry into my life?

2. Where has **Love In Actions**—by others or myself—changed what I believed was possible?

3. What unique, even subtle, moments have helped me discover my voice and my calling to help others?

4. What new beginning is waiting for me if I listen to that inner voice of courage?

Leaving wasn't an ending. It was the beginning of truly reclaiming my FREEDOM, JOY, PEACE, and SELF-LOVE.

> Every step away from fear is a step toward freedom, and every act of self-love creates a ripple of healing for generations.

Chapter Eleven

Living Forward in Love In Actions

Living Forward: Freedom and Legacy

"Freedom is not the end of the story. Once we step into it, we are called to live, to love, and to build a legacy that carries on. Harriet's later years, and my own, show how **Love In Actions** never stops."

Harriet's Story

After years of leading people to freedom and serving as a spy, a nurse and a scout during the Civil War, Harriet Tubman settled in Auburn, New York. Her home became a refuge—doors open, table set for family, neighbors, the poor, and the sick. Even in her eighties, she continued to put love into motion: caring for others, supporting the National Association of Colored Women, speaking for women's rights, and building community.

For Harriet, freedom was never only escape—it was a lifelong practice of dignity, service, and care. She showed us that the call to love does not end when we find freedom; it continues into how we serve, speak, and leave the world for future generations.

One of Harriet's childhood promises to herself, was that she would one day grow apple trees so children after her could eat freely, having once been forced to pick apples but forbidden to eat them herself.

True to her word, she planted an apple orchard in Auburn, sowing not just trees, but a vision of provision and love for generations.

Like Harriet's apple seeds, she planted for the future—not for herself, but for generations yet to come. She would not see the fruit for many years, but her vision and love reached forward in time. This is exactly what GG United by Love is all about.

Think about the power of planting just one apple seed; now imagine the love that any one of us can spread, sow, and grow into entire "love trees" that nourish those who come after us year after year.

My Story

In 2023, my life turned again. In February, my beloved daughter Adia passed at age 47 from cancer. My divorce was final in May, one month before our 48th wedding anniversary. In June, James passed away. In October, my mother, Frances Moss Moore, went home to God at age 101. It was a year marked by heartbreak and loss. However, there were positive times as well.

In January of 2023, I joined Lisa Nichols campus as a member of the Certified Transformational Trainer cohort of 2023. That is where the connections to writing this book started. It is also where I met Melonie Soloway and Zerha Mahoon that I mentioned earlier. *Synchronicities.*

And yet, like Harriet, I kept going by relying on faith, prayer, and **Love In Actions**. Each of their lives contributed to my own journey and remain close to my heart. I believe we come to this world together to be a contributor, supporter, or guide in each other's life—we are here to learn from one another.

James taught me a lot—what self-love is, what it is not, and the deep importance of forgiveness. These lessons, though painful, are now part of the foundation of my freedom. I will share more of what I see as James' part in where I am today, but in future books.

In August of 2023, I drove my dog, a Boston Terrier named Roxxy, and myself back from Ohio to Seattle, WA, a 3,000 mile trip. I moved in with my son Ariessunna and his family. I also met my new husband. July 2025, I remarried to Douglas Jones, an "Earth Angel" who has helped me heal and find new joy.

I am blessed, and committed to living my freedom forward. My heart calls me to uplift women and girls, helping them reclaim their self-love, worth, and freedom. Grandmothers are the most powerful people on earth.

Through self-love and GG United by Love, I see grandmothers reclaiming their inner girl—healing, loving, and leading—one girl at a time, through Love In Actions that transform the world.

Beyond this book, I carry many stories—little books that teach children and adults about self-love, forgiveness, prayer, and the unique ways God calls us to live with **Love In Actions**. I know sharing these stories is part of my purpose: to plant seeds of love that will grow for generations. Now, I know how to share my stories. As I teach from the stories inspired by God's spirit speaking to me, I intertwine my own experiences.

Like Harriet planting her apple orchard, I am planting so that those who come after me may be nourished.

My prayer is that generations to come will live with
Love In Actions, finding freedom, strength, and joy.
And for this purpose, I thank God.

Lesson

Freedom is not a single moment—it is a way of living. Harriet's orchard and my own story of resilience both show that freedom is sustained by faith, forgiveness, service, and love. When we live forward in love, our legacy becomes a blessing for generations.

Reflection Prompts

1. How can I turn my own freedom into a blessing for others?
2. What legacy of love do I want my children and grandchildren to carry forward?
3. Where is God calling me to live out my freedom in action today?

Closing Blessing

May the seeds of love you plant today grow into orchards of freedom, healing, and joy for generations to come.

May your stories, like Harriet Tubman's, light the way. And may we each live forward in Love In Actions.

And so it is, Amen.

Chapter Twelve

GG gets an Upgrade

Synchronicity, Sovereignty, and the Grand Goddess

Part One: Synchronicity and Spirit

Throughout my journey, synchronicities have appeared as gentle nudges—reminders that God's Spirit is guiding me at every turn. The DIVA Network inspired and accelerated the writing and publishing of this book, *Get On Board the Underground Railroad: Harriet Tubman's Spirit is Guiding Us to Love In Actions.*

Each connection, and insight is evidence that when we listen for God's voice, new possibilities and powerful movements are born. Synchronicity, in its truest sense, is not coincidence—it's a divine alignment of events that opens new doors and affirms your path is guided by Spirit. These moments are God's way of whispering, "You're exactly where you're meant to be."

Spirit-Led Connections

I watched *The Secret* movie over and over, then began following Lisa Nichols. These stepping stones led me to the DIVA Network, where a member's book prompted me to face my fears. In this same network, I recently shared my vision for working with grandmothers.

I described starting a membership business—the GG United by Love Club—with a group of younger women. One grandmother in the group didn't like to be called Grandmother or Grandma, and others suggested I should change the name of my club. But I stood firm and explained, "No, this is for grandmothers, because we are often the forgotten women."

That phrase—"Forgotten Women"—instantly resonated with these young ladies. That's how people tend to view grandmothers. I was surprised, yet God's voice nudged me: "Maybe GG deserves an upgrade."

Part Two: Sovereignty and the Grand Goddess
Divine Affirmation: Grandmothers as Grand Goddesses

Think about this. If you agree with the statement, say "true" after each:

God Made Everything
God Loves Everything He(She) Made
God Is Everything He Made
God Doesn't Make Mistakes
There Is Nothing that Is Not God's Creation
When God made people, He loved all of them equally
God made Man
God made Women
God made our Bodies
God Only Makes Beautiful Things
God Made Each of Us Women
God Made Us Mothers
God Made Us Grandmothers
God Made Us Great Grandmothers
Women Are the Female Version of God's Creations He Loves
We Are God's daughters, that makes us "Goddess"
Grandmothers are the GG—**Grand Goddess!**

Don't shy away from being a Grandmother. Be the GG, Grand Goddess that you were born to be! What an honor to be among the most blessed people on Earth. We have witnessed miracles, felt God's love, received divine blessings, and been picked up and carried through storms more than anybody else. But too often, we let others treat us with invisibility, "Forgotten Women".

Why? Because we forget who we are.

Reclaiming Our Sovereignty—New Words to describe Grandmothers (GG)

I have some new words for describing Grandmothers. Another synchronicity: I learned the word *virago* from another beautiful woman in the DIVA Network, Alorah Inanna. And I want to bring back an old favorite—*bodacious.* Let me explain how each of these words, together with *sovereign,* which when describing GG, give GG (Grand Goddess) an upgrade.

Sovereign: To be sovereign is to claim your own inner authority as valid, to live rooted in your truth, and to recognize that you are the ruler of your own life. A sovereign grandmother stands in her wisdom, guided not by external approval, but by inner peace, love, and experience. She leads her family with presence, grace, and the courage to choose joy.

Virago: This word, from the old Latin *virāgō*, once described a woman of exceptional strength, virtue, and courage—a female warrior. Over time, its meaning changed, but I choose to reclaim it in its original power. Grandmothers are modern viragos—protectors, nurturers, teachers, and fierce keepers of the flame.

Every GG carries that Tubman spirit, undaunted, courageous, and full of divine passion.

Bodacious: Rooted in Southern slang, "bodacious" means bold, audacious, and remarkable. A bodacious grandmother lives life out loud!

She is vibrant, fearless, and fun. She doesn't hide her glow; she radiates joy, inspires confidence, and reminds everyone that age is a beautiful gift. The continuing of a life of beauty, not limitation. To be a bodacious GG is to move through the world with faith, flair, and unstoppable love.

These words—**sovereign**, **virago**, and **bodacious**—upgrade what GG stands for. Together they reveal the divine blueprint of the modern Grand Goddess: wise and radiant, fiercely courageous, joyfully bold, and unshakably rooted in love.

Planted Seeds of Love

Love runs the world. It's the love that lifts us after a fall and the love that mothers pass down, generation after generation. Grandmothers are seed planters. Every act of care—every story told, every blessing spoken—is a seed that blooms into beauty and wisdom for those yet to come.

All these expressions of love come from the same source:
the eternal light in your heart, in my heart, and in all of us.

Living in God's House

Now realize: you live in the House of God—your body—and God loves you so deeply that you were made exactly as you asked to be made. He is proud of you. When you live joyfully, when you smile, you look just like Him.

How does that feel? The feeling is what counts. Feel good. Feel worthy. You are here to experience joy.

> In *ACIM*, Lesson 102 says: *God's will for me is perfect happiness.*

Live life as God intended, be grateful for awaking each day to beauty, freedom, and joy.

God wants all of us to feel happy, all the time. If something doesn't feel good, take time alone.

Ask yourself, "Who am I? What do I truly desire?"

Then act in the direction that brings you closer to love and purpose.

I know, like Harriet Tubman must have felt. I know what freedom feels like; joy overflows, when your feet want to move, your heart beats fast, and tears of gratitude pour down your face.

> That feeling is freedom—the freedom to be the Goddess, the Queen, the Grand, GG, **Grand Goddess of Love**. I am proud to say it: I am a GG, a **Grand Goddess of Love.**

What about you?

For me, as I rise to start this membership movement, GG now means *Grand Goddess.* It's a title every grandmother—and every little girl—can aspire to claim one day.

So I invite you—grandmothers, mothers, all women, girls, and yes, men and boys—to get on board the New Underground Railroad!

Let us join hands, hearts, and wisdom, and put our **Love In Ac-**

tions. Let us unite as Grand Goddesses, shining our light together for generations.

Join GG United by Love and be the Grand Goddess, the virago, the bodacious woman who lives in joy, sovereignty, and divine purpose.

Lesson

Synchronicity and sovereignty are invitations to live with divine confidence. They remind us that our lives unfold under God's timing and that our words, choices, and courage become pathways for others to follow. Grandmothers, mothers, and daughters carry this sacred inheritance—**Love In Actions** that ripple through eternity.

Reflection Prompts

1. What synchronicities have appeared in my life recently that remind me I am divinely guided?

2. How have I experienced the sovereignty of my own spirit—when I trusted my inner voice or acted with bold confidence?

3. In what ways can I embody the qualities of the **Virago**—strength, courage, and protection—in my daily life?

4. Where am I called to live more **Bodaciously**—to be bold, creative, and unapologetically joyful?

5. What love seeds am I planting today that will become blessings for future generations?

6. How can I live forward as a radiant, sovereign Grand Goddess of Love—fully aligned with joy, grace, and divine pur-

pose?

7. How am I supporting the women in my life to live in full joy, freedom and appreciation as the Goddess they truly are?

May every synchronicity guide you to step boldly into your sovereignty and shine as the Grand Goddess you were created to be.

Chapter Thirteen

Epilogue: Love in Actions Lives On

Carrying the Torch: Love in Actions

As I close this book, I return to the truth that runs through every chapter: love is not just a feeling, it is an action. It is prayer in motion. It is faith with feet. It is foresight with courage.

Harriet's Torch

Harriet Tubman lived this truth with every breath. She listened for God's voice, trusted her visions, and risked her life again and again to bring others into freedom. I consider her the "Grand Mother of Freedom," loved and honored as a leader, healer, and protector, because she lived with **Love In Actions**.

My Path Forward

My own life has been marked by challenges and heartbreak, but also by grace, faith, and new beginnings. I have learned that self-love is the root of freedom. Without it, we stay silent, fearful, or bound by shame. With it, we rise into courage, compassion, and purpose.

Now, I carry Harriet's torch in my own way—through storytelling, teaching, and lifting up grandmothers, daughters, and children to remember who they are: BELOVED, WORTHY, AND POWERFUL!

You Are the Legacy

You are part of this legacy. Your choices, your stories, your prayers, and your **Love In Actions** will ripple forward into generations yet unborn.

I invite you to plant your seeds of love boldly, through kindness, forgiveness, self-respect, service, and courage. Do not wait for the perfect moment. Do not underestimate the smallest act. Every seed matters.

Harriet planted apple trees so the children who came after her would taste freedom in sweet fruit. I am planting seeds of love so future generations will know they are divine, connected to God and each other and free to live joyful, peaceful lives. And now, it is your turn.

Together, we are building orchards of love. Together, we are writing the next chapter of freedom. Together, we all can step up and say **"I Am Harriet Tubman."**

Affirmation: Say it with me:

I am Harriet Tubman
I am Love In Actions
And so, it is. Amen.

Ways to Keep Love in Actions Alive

1. **Be Grateful:** Appreciate your story and the synchronicities that lead you to this moment in time.

2. **Love YOU: ACIM Lesson 110: I am as God created me.** Say that to yourself every hour of the day.

3. **Listen Deeply:** Be fully present with someone and let them know their story matters.

4. **Speak Up for Justice:** Use your voice to stand with those who are silenced or mistreated.

5. **Give What You Can:** Share your time, talents, or resources generously.

6. **Practice Forgiveness:** Free your spirit from resentment so love can flow again.

7. **Build Generational Bridges:** Share wisdom with young people and receive their wisdom in return.

8. **Don't Worry, Be Happy!:** You are being guided by God.

9. **Get On Board the Love Train, The New Underground Railroad!**

Step forward knowing you are worthy, you are chosen, you are Love In Actions.

Remember: every orchard starts with a single seed and a willing hand. Plant yours boldly.

Chapter Fourteen

Moving Forward Together on the New Underground Railroad

Thank You for Reading

Get On Board the New Underground Railroad, Harriet Tubman's Spirit is Guiding US to Love In Actions

This book is just the beginning of our journey together.

Practice and Share the Vision

Practice the concepts shared in this book.

Discuss this book—use it for family gatherings or community talks.

Purchase copies for your family and friends. Spread the message of **Love In Actions** wherever you go.

Stay Connected with Me

Email: kb4harriettubman@gmail.com

Website: ggunitedbylove.com

Shop for Harriet Tubman Related Gifts: *United By Love Apparel* – available through the website.

Join the Movement

Subscribe to my newsletter and podcast for stories, wisdom, and updates.

Help me bring grandmothers into the movement—purchase a membership for your aunt, friend, mother or grandmother.

Reach out to other women and girls with love, and remind them they are divine and powerful.

Tell and write your stories—I can help you with this!

Invite Me to Speak

I am available to speak and lead workshops on **Love In Actions**, **self-love**, and **intergenerational empowerment**.
Invite me to your church, community center, podcast, or radio program.
Learn more and book me through **ggunitedbylove.com**.

I Have a Gift for You

Access to, "The Harriet Tubman Love In Actions" Movie, my two-hour portrayal of Harriet, now divided into four parts for classroom or group sessions.

You are welcome to watch part 1 for free!
To claim your free download of *The Harriet Tubman Love In Actions Movie, Parts 1.*

1. Count how many times the phrase: ***"I Am Harriet Tubman"*** appears in **Chapter 5 of this book.**

2. Email your answer to **kb4harriettubman@gmail.com**. I will send you a link to the movie.

3. **In your email, give me one thing from this book that sparked love in your heart—I'd love to hear your story.**

4. If you will allow me to share your comments with my community, agree to this in the email.

(If you are interested in the rest of the movie, there are 3 additional parts all about 20 minutes long.)

Together, We Keep the Torch Burning

Your voice, your story, and your **Love In Actions** matter. Together, we will change the world—**one girl, one grandmother, one act of love at a time.**

Blessings,

Karol V. Brown-Jones

(*Hint: the answer is 5.*)

www.ingramcontent.com/pod-product-compliance
Lightning Source LLC
LaVergne TN
LVHW020656100826
845148LV00012B/2522

* 9 7 8 0 9 8 4 0 0 5 0 7 9 *